W9-CRG-862

GRADE 4

Success With
Math Tests

New York • Toronto • London • Auckland • Sydney
Mexico City • New Delhi • Hong Kong • Buenos Aires

Teaching Resources

State Standards Correlations

To find out how this book helps you meet your state's standards, log on to **www.scholastic.com/ssw**

Cover design by Ka-Yeon Kim-Li
Interior illustrations by Kate Flanagan
Interior design by Creative Pages Inc.

ISBN 978-0-545-20065-3

20 21 22   40   24 23 22 21 20

Contents

Introduction

In this book, you will find eight Practice Tests designed to help students prepare to take standardized tests. Each test has 20–30 multiple-choice items that closely resemble the kinds of questions students will have to answer on "real" tests. Each part of the test will take 30–40 minutes for students to complete.

The math skills measured in these tests and the types of questions are based on detailed analyses and correlations with many widely used standardized tests and curriculum standards.

How to Use the Tests

Tell students how much time they will have to complete the test. Encourage students to work quickly and carefully and to keep track of the remaining time—just as they would in a real testing session. You may have students mark their answers directly on the test pages, or you may have them use a copy of the **Answer Sheet**. A copy of the answer sheet appears at the end of each test. The answer sheet will help students become accustomed to filling in bubbles on a real test. It may also make the tests easier for you to score.

We do not recommend the use of calculators. For Practice Tests 2 and 6, students will need an inch ruler and a centimeter ruler to answer some of the questions.

At the back of this book, you will find **Tested Skills** charts and **Answer Keys** for the eight Practice Tests. The Tested Skills charts list the skills measured in each test and the test questions that measure each skill. These charts may be helpful to you in determining what kinds of questions students answered incorrectly, what skills they may be having trouble with, and who may need further instruction in particular skills. To score a Practice Test, refer to the Answer Key for that test. The Answer Key lists the correct response to each question.

To score a Practice Test, go through the test and mark each question answered correctly. Add the total number of questions answered correctly to find the student's test score. To find a percentage score, divide the number answered correctly by the total number of questions. For example, the percentage score for a student who answers 20 out of 25 questions correctly is $20 \div 25 = 0.80$, or 80%. You might want to have students correct their own tests. This will give them a chance to see where they made mistakes and what they need to do to improve their scores on the next test.

On the next page of this book, you will find **Test-Taking Tips**. You may want to share these tips and strategies with students before they begin working on the Practice Tests.

Scholastic Inc.

Test-Taking Tips: Mathematics

1. For each part of the test, read the directions carefully so you know what to do. Then read the directions again—just to make sure.

2. Look for key words and phrases to help you decide what each question is asking and what kind of computation you need to do. Examples of key words: *less than, greatest, least, farther, longest, divided equally.*

3. To help solve a problem, write a number sentence or equation.

4. Use scrap paper (or extra space on the test page) to write down the numbers and information you need to solve a problem.

5. If a question has a picture or diagram, study it carefully. Draw your own picture or diagram if it will help you solve a problem.

6. Try to solve each problem before you look at the answer choices. (In some tests, the correct answer may be "Not Given" or "Not Here," so you will want to be sure of your answer. In these Practice Tests, some of the Math questions use "NG" for "Not Given.")

7. Check your work carefully before you finish. (In many questions, you can check your answer by working backwards to see if the numbers work out correctly.)

8. If you are not sure which answer is correct, cross out every answer that you know is wrong. Then make your best guess.

9. To complete a number sentence or equation, try all the answer choices until you find the one that works.

10. When working with fractions, always reduce (or rename) the fractions to their lowest parts. When working with decimals, keep the decimal points lined up correctly.

Practice
Test 1

Numeration and
Number Concepts

Name Edward   Date _____

Practice Test 1

Directions. Choose the best answer to each question. Mark your answer.

1. The Dent Bridge in Idaho is 1050 feet long. Which words mean 1050?
Ⓐ ten thousand fifty
Ⓑ ten thousand five
Ⓒ one thousand fifty
Ⓓ one hundred fifty

2. What goes in the box to make this number sentence true?

$6 \times 4 = \square$

Ⓕ $6 + 4$
Ⓖ 4×6
Ⓗ $6 - 4$
Ⓙ $6 + 6 + 6 + 6 + 6 + 6$

3. Which river is longest?

Major Rivers of Asia	
Name	**Length (miles)**
Chang	3964
Ganges	1560
Huang	3395
Lena	2734
Ob	2268

Ⓐ Huang
Ⓑ Chang
Ⓒ Lena
Ⓓ Ob

4. What fractional part of this figure is shaded?

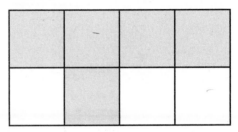

Ⓕ $\dfrac{1}{4}$ Ⓗ $\dfrac{3}{8}$

Ⓖ $\dfrac{3}{5}$ Ⓙ $\dfrac{5}{8}$

5. Which number is equal to $(6 \times 1000) + (4 \times 100) + (5 \times 1)$?

Ⓐ 645   Ⓒ 6405
Ⓑ 6045   Ⓓ 6450

6. Tim has a lemonade stand. The chart shows how much lemonade he sold each day.

Day	Lemonade Sold
Wednesday	$\frac{1}{4}$ gallon
Thursday	$\frac{2}{3}$ gallon
Friday	$\frac{1}{6}$ gallon
Saturday	$\frac{3}{4}$ gallon

On which day did Tim sell the most lemonade?
Ⓕ Wednesday   Ⓗ Friday
Ⓖ Thursday   Ⓙ Saturday

GO ON

Practice Test 1 *(continued)*

7. Which address is an odd number?
- Ⓐ 96 Cole Road
- Ⓑ 48 Main Street
- Ⓒ 20 Brook Road
- Ⓓ 73 Pine Street

8. Which figure shows $\frac{2}{3}$ shaded?

Ⓕ

Ⓗ

Ⓖ

Ⓙ

9. This table shows the number of games won by the Hornets hockey team each year.

Year	2011	2012	2013	2014	2015
Games Won	2	5	8	11	

If this pattern continues, what number should go in the box for 2015?
- Ⓐ 15
- Ⓑ 14
- Ⓒ 13
- Ⓓ 12

This chart lists the highest mountain in each of the six New England states. Use it to answer questions 10 and 11.

Mountains of New England		
State	**Mountain**	**Elevation (feet)**
Connecticut	Frissell	2380
Maine	Katahdin	5267
Massachusetts	Greylock	3487
New Hampshire	Washington	6288
Rhode Island	Jerimoth Hill	812
Vermont	Mansfield	4393

10. The highest mountain is in which state?
- Ⓕ Connecticut
- Ⓖ Maine
- Ⓗ Massachusetts
- Ⓙ New Hampshire

11. Which mountain is taller than Jerimoth Hill but shorter than Greylock?
- Ⓐ Frissell
- Ⓑ Katahdin
- Ⓒ Washington
- Ⓓ Mansfield

GO ON

Practice Test 1 *(continued)*

12. Mr. Barnes drove his truck 4237 miles. What is that number rounded to the nearest hundred?

(F) 4000

(G) 4200

(H) 4300

(J) 5000

13. Claire earned $587 last month. What is that amount rounded to the nearest ten?

(A) $500

(B) $580

(C) $590

(D) $600

14. What goes in the box to make the number sentence true?

$$(3 + 8) + 10 = 3 + (\Box + 10)$$

(F) 6

(G) 7

(H) 8

(J) 10

15. A birthday card costs $1.85. About how much would 300 cards cost?

(A) $30–$40

(B) $50–$60

(C) $300–$400

(D) $500–$600

16. Which number sentence is correct?

(F) $6 \times 0 = 0$

(G) $6 + 0 = 0$

(H) $6 \times 1 = 6 + 1$

(J) $0 \times 6 = 6 \times 1$

17. Sam made this pattern of shapes.

If the pattern continues, what shape should come next?

(A) ○

(B) △

(C) ●

(D) ▲

GO ON

Practice Test 1 *(continued)*

18. Which pair of numbers are factors of 42?

Ⓕ 4, 8

Ⓖ 5, 15

Ⓗ 6, 7

Ⓙ 9, 13

19. The population of Newton is four thousand thirty-five. Which number means four thousand thirty-five?

Ⓐ 4035

Ⓑ 4305

Ⓒ 4350

Ⓓ 40,035

20. Which sign shows an even number?

Ⓕ | Route I-95 |

Ⓖ | 15 Avenue |

Ⓗ | 27 Street |

Ⓙ | Route 128 |

21. What number is equal to $(8 \times 1000) + (7 \times 100) + (2 \times 10)$?

Ⓐ 80,720

Ⓑ 8720

Ⓒ 8702

Ⓓ 8072

22. Randy was thinking of a number with a 9 in the hundreds place. Which of these could be the number?

Ⓕ 5290

Ⓖ 1925

Ⓗ 9137

Ⓙ 2409

23. A total of 7224 people went to the county fair on Saturday, and 4191 people went to the fair on Sunday. Which numbers would give the best estimate of the total number of people at the fair for both days?

Ⓐ 8000 + 4000

Ⓑ 8000 + 5000

Ⓒ 7000 + 5000

Ⓓ 7000 + 4000

Scholastic Inc.

Practice Test 1 *(continued)*

24. Which number sentence goes with $12 - 5 = 7$?

- Ⓕ $7 - 5 = 2$
- Ⓖ $12 + 5 = 17$
- Ⓗ $12 + 7 = 19$
- Ⓙ $5 + 7 = 12$

25. Millie put a total of 465 marbles in 3 boxes. There are 220 marbles in Box 1 and 55 marbles in Box 2. How many marbles are in Box 3?

- Ⓐ 175
- Ⓑ 190
- Ⓒ 275
- Ⓓ 290

26. Last year, the population of Elton was 12,420. Since then, the population has grown by 160 people. Which number sentence should be used to find the total population of Elton now?

- Ⓕ $12,420 \times 160 = \square$
- Ⓖ $12,420 - 160 = \square$
- Ⓗ $12,420 + 160 = \square$
- Ⓙ $12,420 \div 160 = \square$

27. Mr. Clooney sells men's hats. The table shows 4 hats and the size of each hat.

Hat	Size (inches)
1	$7\frac{1}{2}$
2	$8\frac{1}{4}$
3	$6\frac{3}{4}$
4	$7\frac{3}{8}$

Which is the largest hat?
- Ⓐ Hat 1
- Ⓑ Hat 2
- Ⓒ Hat 3
- Ⓓ Hat 4

28. Which figure shows forty-five hundredths shaded?

Ⓕ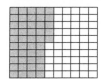

Ⓖ

Ⓗ

Ⓙ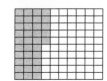

ANSWER SHEET

Practice Test # 1

Student Name _____ Grade _____

Teacher Name _____ Date _____

MATHEMATICS

1 Ⓐ Ⓑ Ⓒ Ⓓ Ⓔ	11 Ⓐ Ⓑ Ⓒ Ⓓ Ⓔ	21 Ⓐ Ⓑ Ⓒ Ⓓ Ⓔ	31 Ⓐ Ⓑ Ⓒ Ⓓ Ⓔ
2 Ⓕ Ⓖ Ⓗ Ⓙ Ⓚ	12 Ⓕ Ⓖ Ⓗ Ⓙ Ⓚ	22 Ⓕ Ⓖ Ⓗ Ⓙ Ⓚ	32 Ⓕ Ⓖ Ⓗ Ⓙ Ⓚ
3 Ⓐ Ⓑ Ⓒ Ⓓ Ⓔ	13 Ⓐ Ⓑ Ⓒ Ⓓ Ⓔ	23 Ⓐ Ⓑ Ⓒ Ⓓ Ⓔ	33 Ⓐ Ⓑ Ⓒ Ⓓ Ⓔ
4 Ⓕ Ⓖ Ⓗ Ⓙ Ⓚ	14 Ⓕ Ⓖ Ⓗ Ⓙ Ⓚ	24 Ⓕ Ⓖ Ⓗ Ⓙ Ⓚ	34 Ⓕ Ⓖ Ⓗ Ⓙ Ⓚ
5 Ⓐ Ⓑ Ⓒ Ⓓ Ⓔ	15 Ⓐ Ⓑ Ⓒ Ⓓ Ⓔ	25 Ⓐ Ⓑ Ⓒ Ⓓ Ⓔ	35 Ⓐ Ⓑ Ⓒ Ⓓ Ⓔ
6 Ⓕ Ⓖ Ⓗ Ⓙ Ⓚ	16 Ⓕ Ⓖ Ⓗ Ⓙ Ⓚ	26 Ⓕ Ⓖ Ⓗ Ⓙ Ⓚ	36 Ⓕ Ⓖ Ⓗ Ⓙ Ⓚ
7 Ⓐ Ⓑ Ⓒ Ⓓ Ⓔ	17 Ⓐ Ⓑ Ⓒ Ⓓ Ⓔ	27 Ⓐ Ⓑ Ⓒ Ⓓ Ⓔ	37 Ⓐ Ⓑ Ⓒ Ⓓ Ⓔ
8 Ⓕ Ⓖ Ⓗ Ⓙ Ⓚ	18 Ⓕ Ⓖ Ⓗ Ⓙ Ⓚ	28 Ⓕ Ⓖ Ⓗ Ⓙ Ⓚ	38 Ⓕ Ⓖ Ⓗ Ⓙ Ⓚ
9 Ⓐ Ⓑ Ⓒ Ⓓ Ⓔ	19 Ⓐ Ⓑ Ⓒ Ⓓ Ⓔ	29 Ⓐ Ⓑ Ⓒ Ⓓ Ⓔ	39 Ⓐ Ⓑ Ⓒ Ⓓ Ⓔ
10 Ⓕ Ⓖ Ⓗ Ⓙ Ⓚ	20 Ⓕ Ⓖ Ⓗ Ⓙ Ⓚ	30 Ⓕ Ⓖ Ⓗ Ⓙ Ⓚ	40 Ⓕ Ⓖ Ⓗ Ⓙ Ⓚ

12 **Scholastic Success With Math Tests • Grade 4**

Practice Test 2

Geometry and Measurement

Practice Test 2

Directions. Choose the best answer to each question. Mark your answer.

1. Which is a rectangle?

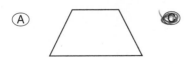
Ⓐ

Ⓒ

Ⓑ

Ⓓ

2. Which figure has exactly 4 faces?

Ⓕ
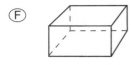

Ⓗ

Ⓖ
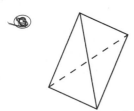

Ⓙ
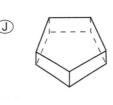

Use the street map below to answer questions 3 and 4.

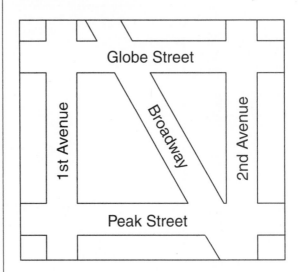

3. Which two streets appear to be parallel?
- Ⓐ 1st Avenue and Peak Street
- Ⓑ Globe Street and Peak Street
- Ⓒ 1st Avenue and Broadway
- Ⓓ Globe Street and 2nd Avenue

4. Which street does *not* intersect with 2nd Avenue?
- Ⓕ 1st Avenue
- Ⓖ Globe Street
- Ⓗ Broadway
- Ⓙ Peak Street

GO ON ⟹

Scholastic Inc.

Practice Test 2 *(continued)*

5. Suppose that each figure can be folded on the dotted line. In which figure are the two parts exactly the same?

 Ⓐ

Ⓒ

Ⓑ

Ⓓ

6. This box will be turned on its side, as shown by the arrow.

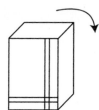

Which picture shows the box turned on its side?

 Ⓕ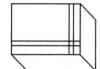

 Ⓗ

 Ⓖ

 Ⓙ

7. Kerry has a rectangular yard for her dogs.

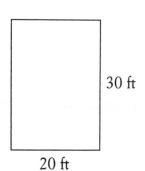

30 ft

20 ft

What is the perimeter of the yard?
Ⓐ 600 ft
Ⓑ 100 ft
Ⓒ 80 ft
Ⓓ 50 ft

8. This picture shows the tiles on Martin's kitchen floor. Each tile is 1 square foot. What is the area of the floor?

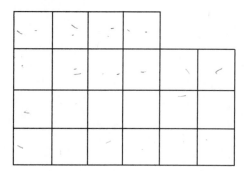

Ⓕ 18 sq ft
Ⓖ 20 sq ft
Ⓗ 22 sq ft
Ⓙ 24 sq ft

GO ON

Practice Test 2 *(continued)*

9. Rico found these coins in his pocket. What is the value of the coins?

- Ⓐ $0.33
- Ⓑ $0.63
- Ⓒ $0.68
- Ⓓ $0.73

10. Stella woke up at 6:25 A.M. Which clock shows the time she woke up?

Ⓕ   Ⓗ

Ⓖ   ⓘ

11. The clock below shows the time when Tomás put a pie in the oven to bake. The pie was done 1 hour 15 minutes later. What time was the pie done?

12:30

- Ⓐ 12:45
- Ⓑ 1:30
- Ⓒ 1:45
- Ⓓ 2:00

12. A family car is most likely to be which length?
- Ⓕ 15 inches
- Ⓖ 15 feet
- Ⓗ 15 yards
- Ⓙ 15 miles

13. Which unit should be used to measure the amount of water in a backyard swimming pool?
- Ⓐ gallons
- Ⓑ pounds
- Ⓒ feet
- Ⓓ ounces

GO ON

Scholastic Inc.

Practice Test 2 *(continued)*

14. This map shows a secret path through the park. What is the length of the path on the map? (Use an inch ruler.)

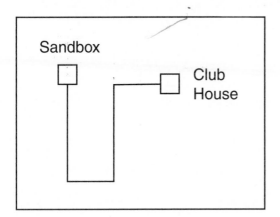

Sandbox

Club House

(F) $1\frac{1}{2}$ in.   (H) $2\frac{1}{2}$ in.

(G) 2 in.   (J) 3 in.

15. How long is the butterfly pin from wing to wing? (Use a centimeter ruler.)

(A) 4 cm

(B) 5 cm

(C) 6 cm

(D) 7 cm

16. What temperature is shown on the thermometer?

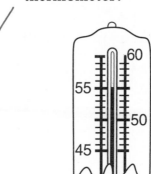

(F) 45°F

(G) 50°F

(H) 55°F

(J) 60°F

17. Mrs. Dolan drove her taxi 285 miles on Monday, 390 miles on Tuesday, and 205 miles on Wednesday. <u>About</u> how far did she drive all together?

(A) 600 miles

(B) 700 miles

(C) 800 miles

(D) 900 miles

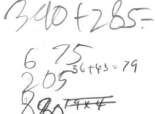

18. Chet earns from $36 to $43 per week on his paper route. <u>About</u> how much does he earn in 4 weeks?

(F) $180

(G) $160

(H) $140

(J) $120

GO ON ➡

Scholastic Inc.

Practice Test 2 *(continued)*

A 4th-grade class is collecting money for a field trip. This bar graph shows how much money the students collected each week. Use the graph to answer questions 19 and 20.

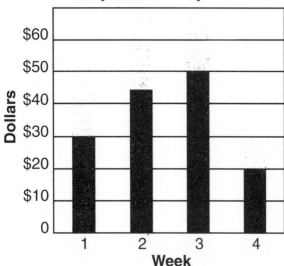

Money Collected by 4th Grade

19. In which week did students collect the most money?
- (A) Week 1
- (B) Week 2
- (C) Week 3
- (D) Week 4

20. How much (more) did students collect in Week 2 than in Week 4?
- (F) $45
- (G) $25
- (H) $15
- (J) $10

Shannon took a survey of 4th graders. She asked students to choose their favorite foods. She made a tally chart to show the results of the survey. Use the chart to answer questions 21 and 22.

Favorite Foods

Mac & Cheese	卌 卌 卌 卌 I
Pizza	卌 卌 IIII
Spaghetti	卌 卌 卌 II
Tacos	卌 卌 卌 卌 III
Hamburger	卌 卌 I

21. Which food was chosen by the greatest number of students?
- (A) Mac & Cheese
- (B) Pizza
- (C) Spaghetti
- (D) Tacos

22. How many students chose spaghetti?
- (F) 17
- (G) 18
- (H) 21
- (J) 23

STOP

ANSWER SHEET

Student Name _____ Grade _____

Teacher Name _____ Date _____

MATHEMATICS

1 Ⓐ Ⓑ Ⓒ Ⓓ Ⓔ	11 Ⓐ Ⓑ Ⓒ Ⓓ Ⓔ	21 Ⓐ Ⓑ Ⓒ Ⓓ Ⓔ	31 Ⓐ Ⓑ Ⓒ Ⓓ Ⓔ
2 Ⓕ Ⓖ Ⓗ Ⓙ Ⓚ	12 Ⓕ Ⓖ Ⓗ Ⓙ Ⓚ	22 Ⓕ Ⓖ Ⓗ Ⓙ Ⓚ	32 Ⓕ Ⓖ Ⓗ Ⓙ Ⓚ
3 Ⓐ Ⓑ Ⓒ Ⓓ Ⓔ	13 Ⓐ Ⓑ Ⓒ Ⓓ Ⓔ	23 Ⓐ Ⓑ Ⓒ Ⓓ Ⓔ	33 Ⓐ Ⓑ Ⓒ Ⓓ Ⓔ
4 Ⓕ Ⓖ Ⓗ Ⓙ Ⓚ	14 Ⓕ Ⓖ Ⓗ Ⓙ Ⓚ	24 Ⓕ Ⓖ Ⓗ Ⓙ Ⓚ	34 Ⓕ Ⓖ Ⓗ Ⓙ Ⓚ
5 Ⓐ Ⓑ Ⓒ Ⓓ Ⓔ	15 Ⓐ Ⓑ Ⓒ Ⓓ Ⓔ	25 Ⓐ Ⓑ Ⓒ Ⓓ Ⓔ	35 Ⓐ Ⓑ Ⓒ Ⓓ Ⓔ
6 Ⓕ Ⓖ Ⓗ Ⓙ Ⓚ	16 Ⓕ Ⓖ Ⓗ Ⓙ Ⓚ	26 Ⓕ Ⓖ Ⓗ Ⓙ Ⓚ	36 Ⓕ Ⓖ Ⓗ Ⓙ Ⓚ
7 Ⓐ Ⓑ Ⓒ Ⓓ Ⓔ	17 Ⓐ Ⓑ Ⓒ Ⓓ Ⓔ	27 Ⓐ Ⓑ Ⓒ Ⓓ Ⓔ	37 Ⓐ Ⓑ Ⓒ Ⓓ Ⓔ
8 Ⓕ Ⓖ Ⓗ Ⓙ Ⓚ	18 Ⓕ Ⓖ Ⓗ Ⓙ Ⓚ	28 Ⓕ Ⓖ Ⓗ Ⓙ Ⓚ	38 Ⓕ Ⓖ Ⓗ Ⓙ Ⓚ
9 Ⓐ Ⓑ Ⓒ Ⓓ Ⓔ	19 Ⓐ Ⓑ Ⓒ Ⓓ Ⓔ	29 Ⓐ Ⓑ Ⓒ Ⓓ Ⓔ	39 Ⓐ Ⓑ Ⓒ Ⓓ Ⓔ
10 Ⓕ Ⓖ Ⓗ Ⓙ Ⓚ	20 Ⓕ Ⓖ Ⓗ Ⓙ Ⓚ	30 Ⓕ Ⓖ Ⓗ Ⓙ Ⓚ	40 Ⓕ Ⓖ Ⓗ Ⓙ Ⓚ

Practice Test 3

Problem Solving

Practice Test 3

Directions. Choose the best answer to each question. Mark your answer. If the correct answer is *not given*, choose "NG."

1. On Saturday, 73 people went to the two o'clock movie at the theater. Each person paid $4.00. How much money did the theater collect in all?

- Ⓐ $332.00
- Ⓑ $292.00
- Ⓒ $146.00
- Ⓓ $18.25
- Ⓔ NG

$$73 \times 4 \over 292$$

2. A total of 84 students are going on a field trip to the science museum. If 8 students can ride in each van, which number sentence should you use to find the number of vans needed for the field trip?

- Ⓕ 84 + 8 = ☐
- Ⓖ 84 − 8 = ☐
- Ⓗ 84 × 8 = ☐
- Ⓙ 84 ÷ 8 = ☐
- Ⓚ NG

3. Mrs. Carver made 345 sandwiches for the school picnic. Students ate 286 of the sandwiches. How many sandwiches were left?

- Ⓐ 41
- Ⓑ 55
- Ⓒ 59
- Ⓓ 69
- Ⓔ NG

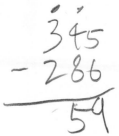

$$345 \over -286 \over 59$$

4. Jeremy uses 6 beads to make a dream catcher. How many dream catchers can he make with 92 beads?

- Ⓕ 12
- Ⓖ 14
- Ⓗ 15
- Ⓙ 16
- Ⓚ NG

exubs

5. Amanda jogged 4.9 miles on Monday and 7.3 miles on Wednesday. How many miles did she jog in all?

- Ⓐ 2.4 miles
- Ⓑ 3.6 miles
- Ⓒ 11.2 miles
- Ⓓ 12.4 miles
- Ⓔ NG

12.

GO ON ⇨

Practice Test 3 *(continued)*

6. Robbie bought this jacket in a department store. He gave the clerk a $20.00 bill.

$16.95

How much change should Robbie get back?

20.00
−16.95
4.05

Ⓕ $2.95
Ⓖ $3.05
Ⓗ $3.15
Ⓙ $4.05
Ⓚ NG

7. Selena was 4 ft 10 in. last year. Since then she has grown 3 inches. How tall is she now?

Ⓐ 4 ft 7 in.
Ⓑ 4 ft 11 in.
Ⓒ 5 ft 2 in.
Ⓓ 5 ft 3 in.
Ⓔ NG

8. Bilbo has these marbles in his collection.

Bilbo's Marbles	
Cat's eye	105
Aggies	62
Glass	47

How many marbles does he have in all?

167
204

Ⓕ 104
Ⓖ 114
Ⓗ 204
Ⓙ 214
Ⓚ NG

9. Mr. Breen bought $1\frac{1}{2}$ pounds of cake flour and $2\frac{1}{2}$ pounds of bread flour. How much flour did he buy all together?

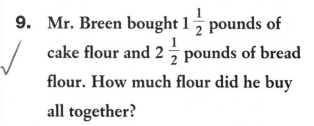

Cake Flour
$1\frac{1}{2}$ lb

Bread Flour
$2\frac{1}{2}$ lb

Ⓐ 3 lb
Ⓑ $3\frac{1}{2}$ lb
Ⓒ 4 lb
Ⓓ $4\frac{1}{2}$ lb
Ⓔ NG

GO ON

Practice Test 3 *(continued)*

10. Git works 28 hours each week. He worked 7 hours on Monday and 6 hours on Tuesday. How many more hours does he have to work this week?

- Ⓕ 41
- Ⓖ 22
- Ⓗ 21
- ⬤ 15
- Ⓚ NG

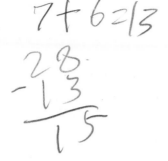

$7 + 6 = 13$

$\begin{array}{r} 28 \\ -13 \\ \hline 15 \end{array}$

11. Nina fell asleep on the sofa at 4:15 P.M. She woke up at 5:45 P.M. How long did she sleep?

- Ⓐ 1 hr 15 min
- ⬤ 1 hr 30 min
- Ⓒ 1 hr 45 min
- Ⓓ 2 hr
- Ⓔ NG

12. Dan rode his bicycle across the United States. The trip took 64 days. How many weeks did the trip last?

- Ⓕ 6 weeks 4 days
- Ⓖ 8 weeks 6 days
- Ⓗ 9 weeks 1 day
- Ⓙ 10 weeks
- ⬤ NG

2

$24)\overline{64}$

13. A puppy named Max weighs 12 pounds. Max gains 2 pounds per week. At this rate, how much will Max weigh in 3 weeks?

- Ⓐ 14 lb
- Ⓑ 15 lb
- Ⓒ 17 lb
- ⬤ 18 lb
- Ⓔ NG

14. Clem scored 34 points in a basketball game. Leo scored 26 points. Which number sentence should you use to find how many more points Clem scored?

- Ⓕ 26 + 34 = ☐
- Ⓖ 26 − 34 = ☐
- Ⓗ 34 × 26 = ☐
- Ⓙ 34 ÷ 26 = ☐
- ⬤ NG

15. Buzzy started watching a video at 9:30 A.M. The video lasted 80 minutes. At what time did the video end?

- Ⓐ 9:50 A.M.
- Ⓑ 10:30 A.M.
- Ⓒ 10:40 A.M.
- ⬤ 10:50 A.M.
- Ⓔ NG

GO ON ⟩

Practice Test 3 (continued)

16. If you spin the spinner 20 times, which number will the spinner probably land on most often?

- Ⓕ 2
- Ⓖ 3
- Ⓗ 4
- Ⓙ 5
- Ⓚ NG

17. At Joe's Adventure Golf, golf balls are kept in a large box. The chart shows how many balls of each color are in the box.

Color	Number
Red	24
Blue	12
Yellow	68
Green	20
Purple	35

If you reach into the box without looking and take one golf ball, which color are you most likely to get?

- Ⓐ red
- Ⓑ blue
- Ⓒ yellow
- Ⓓ green
- Ⓔ NG

18. Keith uses 5 lemons to make 2 pitchers of lemonade.

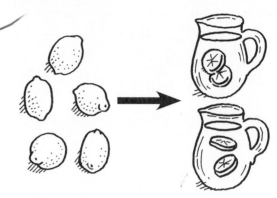

At this rate, how many lemons would Keith use to make 12 pitchers of lemonade?

- Ⓕ 12
- Ⓖ 15
- Ⓗ 20
- Ⓙ 30
- Ⓚ NG

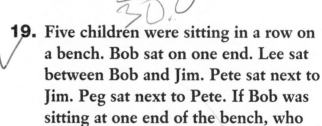

19. Five children were sitting in a row on a bench. Bob sat on one end. Lee sat between Bob and Jim. Pete sat next to Jim. Peg sat next to Pete. If Bob was sitting at one end of the bench, who was sitting at the other end?

- Ⓐ Peg
- Ⓑ Lee
- Ⓒ Pete
- Ⓓ Jim
- Ⓔ NG

GO ON

Practice Test 3 *(continued)*

20. Carla had $100. She spent $32.00 on groceries and $26.00 for gasoline. How much money did she have left?

 Ⓕ $42.00
 Ⓖ $58.00
 Ⓗ $68.00
 Ⓙ $74.00
 Ⓚ   NG

$32 + 26 = 58$

21. Mr. Harrison drove 1150 miles in March, 2180 miles in April, and 1937 miles in May. <u>About</u> how many miles in all did he drive in these 3 months?

 Ⓐ   3,000
 Ⓑ   4,000
 Ⓒ   5,000
 Ⓓ   6,000

$$1150$$
$$+ 1,937$$
$$\overline{3087}$$
$$+ 2,180$$
$$\overline{5267}$$

22. Sam bought 50 stamps for $0.34 each. <u>About</u> how much did he spend on stamps?

 Ⓕ $1.50–$2.00
 Ⓖ $5.00–$8.00
 Ⓗ $15.00–$20.00
 Ⓙ $150.00–$200.00

Great !

23. Members of the Kids' Club held a car wash one day to make money. They washed 74 cars in all. What else do you need to know to figure out how much money they made?

 Ⓐ   how much they charged for each car
 Ⓑ   what day the car wash was held
 Ⓒ   how many members are in the club
 Ⓓ   where the car wash was held
 Ⓔ   NG

24. Sharon saved $620 last year. Her sister Kayla saved $75.00 less than that. How much did Kayla save?

 Ⓕ $535
 Ⓖ $545
 Ⓗ $555
 Ⓙ $695
 Ⓚ   NG

$$620$$
$$- \;75$$
$$\overline{545}$$

25. Grace is reading a book that is 260 pages long. She read 24 pages on Monday, 30 pages on Tuesday, and 25 pages on Wednesday. How many pages does she have left to read?

 Ⓐ   79
 Ⓑ   181
 Ⓒ   206
 Ⓓ   230
 Ⓔ   NG

$$24$$
$$+30$$
$$\overline{54}$$
$$+25$$
$$\overline{79}$$

$$260$$
$$- \;79$$
$$\overline{181}$$

STOP

Student Name _____ Grade _____

Teacher Name _____ Date _____

MATHEMATICS

1 Ⓐ Ⓑ Ⓒ Ⓓ Ⓔ	**11** Ⓐ Ⓑ Ⓒ Ⓓ Ⓔ	**21** Ⓐ Ⓑ Ⓒ Ⓓ Ⓔ	**31** Ⓐ Ⓑ Ⓒ Ⓓ Ⓔ
2 Ⓕ Ⓖ Ⓗ Ⓙ Ⓚ	**12** Ⓕ Ⓖ Ⓗ Ⓙ Ⓚ	**22** Ⓕ Ⓖ Ⓗ Ⓙ Ⓚ	**32** Ⓕ Ⓖ Ⓗ Ⓙ Ⓚ
3 Ⓐ Ⓑ Ⓒ Ⓓ Ⓔ	**13** Ⓐ Ⓑ Ⓒ Ⓓ Ⓔ	**23** Ⓐ Ⓑ Ⓒ Ⓓ Ⓔ	**33** Ⓐ Ⓑ Ⓒ Ⓓ Ⓔ
4 Ⓕ Ⓖ Ⓗ Ⓙ Ⓚ	**14** Ⓕ Ⓖ Ⓗ Ⓙ Ⓚ	**24** Ⓕ Ⓖ Ⓗ Ⓙ Ⓚ	**34** Ⓕ Ⓖ Ⓗ Ⓙ Ⓚ
5 Ⓐ Ⓑ Ⓒ Ⓓ Ⓔ	**15** Ⓐ Ⓑ Ⓒ Ⓓ Ⓔ	**25** Ⓐ Ⓑ Ⓒ Ⓓ Ⓔ	**35** Ⓐ Ⓑ Ⓒ Ⓓ Ⓔ
6 Ⓕ Ⓖ Ⓗ Ⓙ Ⓚ	**16** Ⓕ Ⓖ Ⓗ Ⓙ Ⓚ	**26** Ⓕ Ⓖ Ⓗ Ⓙ Ⓚ	**36** Ⓕ Ⓖ Ⓗ Ⓙ Ⓚ
7 Ⓐ Ⓑ Ⓒ Ⓓ Ⓔ	**17** Ⓐ Ⓑ Ⓒ Ⓓ Ⓔ	**27** Ⓐ Ⓑ Ⓒ Ⓓ Ⓔ	**37** Ⓐ Ⓑ Ⓒ Ⓓ Ⓔ
8 Ⓕ Ⓖ Ⓗ Ⓙ Ⓚ	**18** Ⓕ Ⓖ Ⓗ Ⓙ Ⓚ	**28** Ⓕ Ⓖ Ⓗ Ⓙ Ⓚ	**38** Ⓕ Ⓖ Ⓗ Ⓙ Ⓚ
9 Ⓐ Ⓑ Ⓒ Ⓓ Ⓔ	**19** Ⓐ Ⓑ Ⓒ Ⓓ Ⓔ	**29** Ⓐ Ⓑ Ⓒ Ⓓ Ⓔ	**39** Ⓐ Ⓑ Ⓒ Ⓓ Ⓔ
10 Ⓕ Ⓖ Ⓗ Ⓙ Ⓚ	**20** Ⓕ Ⓖ Ⓗ Ⓙ Ⓚ	**30** Ⓕ Ⓖ Ⓗ Ⓙ Ⓚ	**40** Ⓕ Ⓖ Ⓗ Ⓙ Ⓚ

Practice
Test 4

Computation

22/28

Practice Test 4

Directions. Choose the best answer to each question. Mark your answer. If the correct answer is *not given,* choose "NG."

1.

$$\begin{array}{r} 317 \\ 84 \\ + 129 \\ \hline \end{array}$$

530

- (A) 420
- (B) 430
- (C) 510
- (D) 530
- (E) NG

2.

$$\begin{array}{r} 602 \\ - 51 \\ \hline 551 \end{array}$$

- (F) 653
- (G) 651
- (H) 553
- (J) 541
- (K) NG

3.

$$\begin{array}{r} 487 \\ - 219 \\ \hline 268 \end{array}$$

- (A) 252
- (B) 262
- (C) 268
- (D) 278
- (E) NG

4. This chart shows the number of pies sold each day at a bakery.

Pies Sold	
Tuesday	8
Wednesday	12
Thursday	20
Friday	24

What was the average number of pies sold each day?

- (F) 12
- (G) 16
- (H) 24
- (J) 64
- (K) NG

20
40
64
16
32

5. Mr. James took 3 flights this week.

Flight	Distance (miles)
Seattle–Salem	212
Salem–Boise	433
Boise–Seattle	487

How many miles did he fly in all?

- (A) 1122
- (B) 1132
- (C) 1222
- (D) 1232
- (E) NG

645
1132

GO ON

Scholastic Inc.

Practice Test 4 *(continued)*

6.
$$\begin{array}{r} 75 \\ \times\ 4 \\ \hline 300 \end{array}$$

- Ⓕ 260
- Ⓖ 275
- Ⓗ 280
- Ⓙ 300
- Ⓚ NG

7.
$$\begin{array}{r} 519 \\ \times\ 3 \\ \hline 1557 \end{array}$$

- Ⓐ 1554
- Ⓑ 1547
- Ⓒ 1537
- Ⓓ 1534
- Ⓔ NG

8.
$$\begin{array}{r} 60 \\ \times\ 20 \\ \hline \end{array}$$

- Ⓕ 120
- Ⓖ 800
- Ⓗ 1200
- Ⓙ 1220
- Ⓚ NG

9. $8 \times \square = 56$

- Ⓐ 5
- Ⓑ 6
- Ⓒ 7
- Ⓓ 8
- Ⓔ NG

10. Paul has 4 different colored T-shirts and 2 pairs of shorts.

4   2

How many different combinations of one T-shirt and a pair of shorts can he wear?

- Ⓕ 12
- Ⓖ 8
- Ⓗ 6
- Ⓙ 4
- Ⓚ NG

11. Lena has these hair ties in a drawer.

Color	Number
Red	4
Yellow	5
Black	8
White	3

If Lena takes one hair tie out of the drawer without looking, what is the probability that she will choose a yellow one?

- Ⓐ $\dfrac{1}{4}$
- Ⓑ $\dfrac{5}{10}$
- Ⓒ $\dfrac{1}{20}$
- Ⓓ $\dfrac{1}{5}$
- Ⓔ NG

$\dfrac{5}{20} = \dfrac{4}{4}$

GO ON

Practice Test 4 (continued)

12. $32 \div 4 =$

- Ⓕ 4
- Ⓖ 6
- Ⓗ 7
- Ⓙ 9
- Ⓚ NG

13. $7\overline{)63}$

- Ⓐ 7
- Ⓑ 8
- Ⓒ 9
- Ⓓ 11
- Ⓔ NG

14. $4\overline{)84}$

- Ⓕ 20
- Ⓖ 21
- Ⓗ 22
- Ⓙ 31
- Ⓚ NG

15. $3\overline{)960}$

- Ⓐ 32
- Ⓑ 310
- Ⓒ 318
- Ⓓ 320
- Ⓔ NG

16. The grid shows where five points are located.

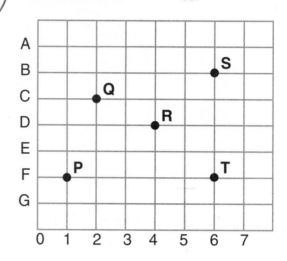

Which point is located at 6B?

- Ⓕ point P
- Ⓖ point Q
- Ⓗ point R
- Ⓙ point S
- Ⓚ NG

17. Ms. Teplick wrote this number sentence on the blackboard.

$$(16 + n) - 5 = 30$$

What is the value of *n*?

- Ⓐ 19
- Ⓑ 20
- Ⓒ 29
- Ⓓ 35
- Ⓔ NG

GO ON

Scholastic Inc.

Practice Test 4 *(continued)*

18. This chart shows the number of books students read in the summer reading program.

Books Read	
Megan	15
Carl	6
Trudy	9
Ronnie	10

What was the average number of books read per student?

ⓕ 40
ⓖ 15
Ⓗ 10
ⓙ 9
Ⓚ NG

21
30
40

19. Harry wrote this number sentence to solve a problem.

$$(8 \times n) - 4 = 20$$

What is the value of *n*?

Ⓐ 2
Ⓑ 4
Ⓒ 6
Ⓓ 8
Ⓔ NG

The grid below shows the location of six shapes. Use the grid to answer questions 20 and 21.

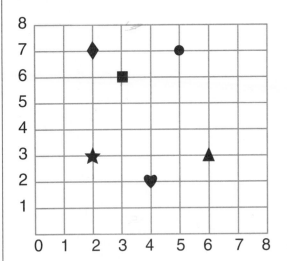

20. What shape is located at (6, 3)?

ⓕ ♥
Ⓖ ▲
Ⓗ ★
ⓙ ■
Ⓚ NG

21. What is the location of the ◆ ?

Ⓐ (7, 2)
Ⓑ (3, 6)
Ⓒ (2, 3)
Ⓓ (2, 7)
Ⓔ NG

GO ON

Practice Test 4 *(continued)*

22. $\frac{3}{5} + \frac{1}{5} =$

    F $\frac{3}{5}$

    G $\frac{3}{25}$

    H $\frac{4}{5}$

    J $\frac{4}{10}$

    K   NG

25. $4.5 + 7.1 =$

    A   12.6

    B   11.6

    C   10.6

    D   2.6

    E   NG

26. $13.28 + 9.7 =$

    F   21.98

    G   22.35

    H   22.88

    J   23.08

    K   NG

$$13.28$$
$$+\ 9.7$$
$$\overline{22.98}$$

23.

$$\begin{array}{r} \frac{1}{8} \\ + \frac{5}{8} \\ \hline \end{array}$$

    A $\frac{3}{4}$

    B $\frac{4}{8}$

    C $\frac{6}{16}$

    D $\frac{3}{8}$

    E   NG

27. $\$13.00 - \$5.49 =$

    A $\$8.59$

    B $\$8.49$

    C $\$7.91$

    D $\$7.51$

    E   NG

24.

$$\begin{array}{r} \frac{9}{10} \\ - \frac{3}{10} \\ \hline \end{array}$$

    F $1\frac{2}{10}$

    G $\frac{3}{5}$

    H $\frac{6}{20}$

    J $\frac{5}{10}$

    K   NG

28. $24.05 - 16.8 =$

    F   8.30

    G   8.03

    H   7.70

    J   7.25

    K   NG

Scholastic Inc.

ANSWER SHEET

Student Name _____ Grade _____

Teacher Name _____ Date _____

MATHEMATICS

1 Ⓐ Ⓑ Ⓒ Ⓓ Ⓔ   11 Ⓐ Ⓑ Ⓒ Ⓓ Ⓔ   21 Ⓐ Ⓑ Ⓒ Ⓓ Ⓔ   31 Ⓐ Ⓑ Ⓒ Ⓓ Ⓔ

2 Ⓕ Ⓖ Ⓗ Ⓙ Ⓚ   12 Ⓕ Ⓖ Ⓗ Ⓙ Ⓚ   22 Ⓕ Ⓖ Ⓗ Ⓙ Ⓚ   32 Ⓕ Ⓖ Ⓗ Ⓙ Ⓚ

3 Ⓐ Ⓑ Ⓒ Ⓓ Ⓔ   13 Ⓐ Ⓑ Ⓒ Ⓓ Ⓔ   23 Ⓐ Ⓑ Ⓒ Ⓓ Ⓔ   33 Ⓐ Ⓑ Ⓒ Ⓓ Ⓔ

4 Ⓕ Ⓖ Ⓗ Ⓙ Ⓚ   14 Ⓕ Ⓖ Ⓗ Ⓙ Ⓚ   24 Ⓕ Ⓖ Ⓗ Ⓙ Ⓚ   34 Ⓕ Ⓖ Ⓗ Ⓙ Ⓚ

5 Ⓐ Ⓑ Ⓒ Ⓓ Ⓔ   15 Ⓐ Ⓑ Ⓒ Ⓓ Ⓔ   25 Ⓐ Ⓑ Ⓒ Ⓓ Ⓔ   35 Ⓐ Ⓑ Ⓒ Ⓓ Ⓔ

6 Ⓕ Ⓖ Ⓗ Ⓙ Ⓚ   16 Ⓕ Ⓖ Ⓗ Ⓙ Ⓚ   26 Ⓕ Ⓖ Ⓗ Ⓙ Ⓚ   36 Ⓕ Ⓖ Ⓗ Ⓙ Ⓚ

7 Ⓐ Ⓑ Ⓒ Ⓓ Ⓔ   17 Ⓐ Ⓑ Ⓒ Ⓓ Ⓔ   27 Ⓐ Ⓑ Ⓒ Ⓓ Ⓔ   37 Ⓐ Ⓑ Ⓒ Ⓓ Ⓔ

8 Ⓕ Ⓖ Ⓗ Ⓙ Ⓚ   18 Ⓕ Ⓖ Ⓗ Ⓙ Ⓚ   28 Ⓕ Ⓖ Ⓗ Ⓙ Ⓚ   38 Ⓕ Ⓖ Ⓗ Ⓙ Ⓚ

9 Ⓐ Ⓑ Ⓒ Ⓓ Ⓔ   19 Ⓐ Ⓑ Ⓒ Ⓓ Ⓔ   29 Ⓐ Ⓑ Ⓒ Ⓓ Ⓔ   39 Ⓐ Ⓑ Ⓒ Ⓓ Ⓔ

10 Ⓕ Ⓖ Ⓗ Ⓙ Ⓚ   20 Ⓕ Ⓖ Ⓗ Ⓙ Ⓚ   30 Ⓕ Ⓖ Ⓗ Ⓙ Ⓚ   40 Ⓕ Ⓖ Ⓗ Ⓙ Ⓚ

Practice Test 5

Numeration and Number Concepts

Practice Test 5

Directions. Choose the best answer to each question. Mark your answer.

1. The highest mountain in Kansas is 4039 feet. Which words mean 4039?

Ⓐ forty thousand thirty-nine
Ⓑ four thousand thirty-nine
Ⓒ four thousand three hundred nine
Ⓓ four hundred thirty-nine

2. What goes in the box to make this number sentence true?

$7 \times 3 = \square$

Ⓕ 3×7
Ⓖ $7 + 3$
Ⓗ $7 \div 3$
Ⓙ $7 - 3$

3. Which basketball player made the most free throws?

Name	Free Throws Made
Jamal	2135
Derrick	3818
Scott	3445
Calvin	1548
Stephen	3960

Ⓐ Jamal
Ⓑ Derrick
Ⓒ Scott
Ⓓ Stephen

4. What fractional part of this figure is shaded?

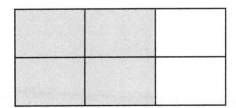

Ⓕ $\dfrac{5}{6}$ Ⓗ $\dfrac{2}{3}$
Ⓖ $\dfrac{1}{2}$ Ⓙ $\dfrac{2}{4}$

5. Which number is equal to $(3 \times 1000) + (8 \times 100) + (9 \times 1)$?

Ⓐ 389 Ⓒ 3809
Ⓑ 3089 Ⓓ 3890

6. The chart shows how much maple syrup Chad made one week.

Day	Maple Syrup Made
Sunday	$\frac{1}{2}$ gallon
Tuesday	$\frac{3}{4}$ gallon
Thursday	$\frac{5}{8}$ gallon
Saturday	$\frac{1}{3}$ gallon

On which day did Chad make the most syrup?

Ⓕ Sunday Ⓗ Thursday
Ⓖ Tuesday Ⓙ Saturday

GO ON

Practice Test 5 *(continued)*

7. Which address is an even number?

- (A) 84 Lemon Road
- (B) 75 Elm Street
- (C) 99 Fifth Street
- (D) 61 Morgan Road

8. Which figure shows $\frac{3}{5}$ shaded?

9. This table shows the number of points Josh scored in each basketball game.

Game	1	2	3	4	5	6
Points	7	12	17	22	27	

If this pattern continues, what number should go in the box for Game 6?

- (A) 29
- (B) 30
- (C) 32
- (D) 37

This chart lists the length of the shoreline in each of six states. Use the chart to answer questions 10 and 11.

Shoreline of U.S. States	
State	**Shoreline (miles)**
Georgia	2344
Maine	3478
Maryland	3190
Massachusetts	1519
New Jersey	1792
Virginia	2876

10. Which of these states has the longest shoreline?

- (F) Georgia
- (G) Maine
- (H) Maryland
- (J) Virginia

11. Which state has a longer shoreline than Massachusetts but shorter than Georgia?

- (A) Maryland
- (B) Maine
- (C) Virginia
- (D) New Jersey

GO ON ⇨

Practice Test 5 (continued)

12. Ms. Falco paid $8675 for rent last year. What is that amount rounded to the nearest hundred dollars?

   Ⓕ $8000

   Ⓖ $8600

   Ⓗ $8700

   Ⓙ $9000

13. Stella drove 607 miles last week. What is that number rounded to the nearest ten?

   Ⓐ   700

   Ⓑ   650

   Ⓒ   610

   Ⓓ   600

14. What goes in the box to make the number sentence true?

$$(16 + 4) + 5 = (4 + 5) + \square$$

   Ⓕ   7

   Ⓖ   10

   Ⓗ   12

   Ⓙ   16

15. A new book costs $19.95. <u>About</u> how much would 50 of these books cost?

   Ⓐ $70–$80

   Ⓑ $90–$100

   Ⓒ $700–$800

   Ⓓ $900–$1000

16. Which number sentence is correct?

   Ⓕ $1 \times 5 = 15$

   Ⓖ $5 \times 0 = 0$

   Ⓗ $5 \times 1 = 5 + 1$

   Ⓙ $0 \times 5 = 5 \times 1$

17. Hal made this pattern of shapes

If the pattern continues, what shape should come next?

   Ⓐ   ▢

   Ⓑ   ⇨

   Ⓒ   ◇

   Ⓓ   ⇦

GO ON

Practice Test 5 *(continued)*

18. Which pair of numbers are factors of 56?

(F) 7, 8

(G) 4, 12

(H) 9, 6

(J) 5, 11

19. The Allegheny Tunnel in Pennsylvania is six thousand seventy-two feet long. Which number means six thousand seventy-two?

(A) 672

(B) 6072

(C) 6720

(D) 60,072

20. Which ZIP code is an odd number?

(F) 97420

(G) 22308

(H) 15501

(J) 78336

21. What number is equal to $(4 \times 1000) + (9 \times 100) + (7 \times 10)$?

(A) 40,970

(B) 4907

(C) 4097

(D) 4970

22. Which number has a 5 in the thousands place?

(F) 2415

(G) 3580

(H) 5721

(J) 8350

23. A total of 6120 people went to the zoo on Saturday to see the pandas, and 8870 went on Sunday. Which numbers would give the best estimate of the total number of people who went to the zoo for both days?

(A) 6000 + 8000

(B) 7000 + 8000

(C) 6000 + 9000

(D) 7000 + 9000

GO ON

Scholastic Inc.

Practice Test 5 *(continued)*

24. Which fact is in the same family as
9 − 4 = 5?

  Ⓕ   5 + 4 = 9

  Ⓖ   9 + 5 = 14

  Ⓗ   9 + 4 = 13

  Ⓙ   5 − 4 = 1

25. The numbers 3, 6, and 9 are all factors
of what number?

  Ⓐ   18

  Ⓑ   24

  Ⓒ   27

  Ⓓ   30

26. Which figure shows thirty-six
hundredths shaded?

  Ⓕ

  Ⓖ

  Ⓗ

  Ⓙ

27. Mr. James wanted to buy a barrel.
He compared how many gallons of
water each barrel could hold.

Barrel	Capacity (gal)
1	$18\frac{3}{4}$
2	$17\frac{9}{10}$
3	$18\frac{1}{3}$
4	$17\frac{7}{8}$

Which barrel holds the most?

  Ⓐ   Barrel 1

  Ⓑ   Barrel 2

  Ⓒ   Barrel 3

  Ⓓ   Barrel 4

28. Four people won a prize of $10,500.
Each person will get an equal share
of the prize. Which number sentence
should be used to find the amount
that each person should get?

  Ⓕ $10,500 × 4 = ☐

  Ⓖ $10,500 + 4 = ☐

  Ⓗ $10,500 − 4 = ☐

  Ⓙ $10,500 ÷ 4 = ☐

STOP

ANSWER SHEET

Student Name _____ Grade _____

Teacher Name _____ Date _____

MATHEMATICS

1 Ⓐ Ⓑ Ⓒ Ⓓ Ⓔ	11 Ⓐ Ⓑ Ⓒ Ⓓ Ⓔ	21 Ⓐ Ⓑ Ⓒ Ⓓ Ⓔ	31 Ⓐ Ⓑ Ⓒ Ⓓ Ⓔ
2 Ⓕ Ⓖ Ⓗ Ⓙ Ⓚ	12 Ⓕ Ⓖ Ⓗ Ⓙ Ⓚ	22 Ⓕ Ⓖ Ⓗ Ⓙ Ⓚ	32 Ⓕ Ⓖ Ⓗ Ⓙ Ⓚ
3 Ⓐ Ⓑ Ⓒ Ⓓ Ⓔ	13 Ⓐ Ⓑ Ⓒ Ⓓ Ⓔ	23 Ⓐ Ⓑ Ⓒ Ⓓ Ⓔ	33 Ⓐ Ⓑ Ⓒ Ⓓ Ⓔ
4 Ⓕ Ⓖ Ⓗ Ⓙ Ⓚ	14 Ⓕ Ⓖ Ⓗ Ⓙ Ⓚ	24 Ⓕ Ⓖ Ⓗ Ⓙ Ⓚ	34 Ⓕ Ⓖ Ⓗ Ⓙ Ⓚ
5 Ⓐ Ⓑ Ⓒ Ⓓ Ⓔ	15 Ⓐ Ⓑ Ⓒ Ⓓ Ⓔ	25 Ⓐ Ⓑ Ⓒ Ⓓ Ⓔ	35 Ⓐ Ⓑ Ⓒ Ⓓ Ⓔ
6 Ⓕ Ⓖ Ⓗ Ⓙ Ⓚ	16 Ⓕ Ⓖ Ⓗ Ⓙ Ⓚ	26 Ⓕ Ⓖ Ⓗ Ⓙ Ⓚ	36 Ⓕ Ⓖ Ⓗ Ⓙ Ⓚ
7 Ⓐ Ⓑ Ⓒ Ⓓ Ⓔ	17 Ⓐ Ⓑ Ⓒ Ⓓ Ⓔ	27 Ⓐ Ⓑ Ⓒ Ⓓ Ⓔ	37 Ⓐ Ⓑ Ⓒ Ⓓ Ⓔ
8 Ⓕ Ⓖ Ⓗ Ⓙ Ⓚ	18 Ⓕ Ⓖ Ⓗ Ⓙ Ⓚ	28 Ⓕ Ⓖ Ⓗ Ⓙ Ⓚ	38 Ⓕ Ⓖ Ⓗ Ⓙ Ⓚ
9 Ⓐ Ⓑ Ⓒ Ⓓ Ⓔ	19 Ⓐ Ⓑ Ⓒ Ⓓ Ⓔ	29 Ⓐ Ⓑ Ⓒ Ⓓ Ⓔ	39 Ⓐ Ⓑ Ⓒ Ⓓ Ⓔ
10 Ⓕ Ⓖ Ⓗ Ⓙ Ⓚ	20 Ⓕ Ⓖ Ⓗ Ⓙ Ⓚ	30 Ⓕ Ⓖ Ⓗ Ⓙ Ⓚ	40 Ⓕ Ⓖ Ⓗ Ⓙ Ⓚ

Practice
Test 6

Geometry and Measurement

Practice Test 6

Directions. Choose the best answer to each question. Mark your answer.

1. Which sign is a triangle?

Ⓐ    Ⓒ

Ⓑ 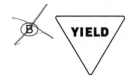   Ⓓ

2. Which figure has exactly 6 faces?

Ⓕ 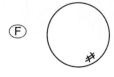   Ⓗ

Ⓖ 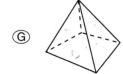   Ⓙ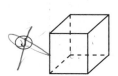

3. Which figure has only two sides that are parallel?

Ⓐ 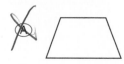   Ⓒ

Ⓑ 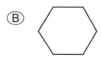   Ⓓ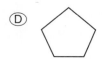

4. In which pair are the figures congruent? = the same

Ⓕ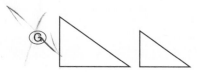

Ⓖ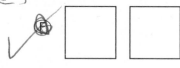

Ⓗ

Ⓙ

GO ON ⇨

Practice Test 6 *(continued)*

Use the map below to answer questions 5 and 6.

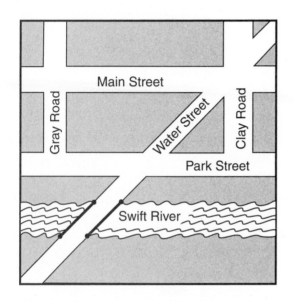

5. Which street intersects with the Swift River?
- Ⓐ Main Street
- ~~Ⓑ~~ Water Street
- Ⓒ Park Street
- Ⓓ Gray Road

6. Which street is parallel to Main Street?
- Ⓕ Gray Road
- Ⓖ Water Street
- ~~Ⓗ~~ Park Street
- Ⓙ Clay Road

The bar graph below shows the number of books sold by the Peter Pan Book Shop each week. Use the graph to answer questions 7 and 8.

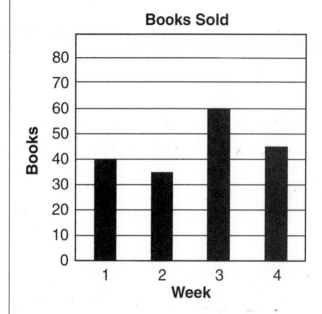

7. How many books were sold in Week 2?
- Ⓐ 45
- Ⓑ 40
- ~~Ⓒ~~ 35
- Ⓓ 30

8. How many more books were sold in Week 3 than in Week 4?
- Ⓕ 5
- Ⓖ 10
- ~~Ⓗ~~ 15
- Ⓙ 20

GO ON

Practice Test 6 *(continued)*

9. Which letter has a line of symmetry?

Ⓐ H   Ⓒ J

Ⓑ G   Ⓓ F

10. A rectangular parking lot measures 80 meters by 25 meters.

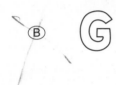

25 m

80 m

What is the perimeter of the parking lot?

Ⓕ 105 m
Ⓖ 210 m
Ⓗ 420 m
Ⓙ 2000 m

50

160

11. Which unit should be used to measure the height of a house?

Ⓐ inches
Ⓑ gallons
Ⓒ pounds
Ⓓ feet

12. This flag will be flipped to the other side of the pole when the wind changes.

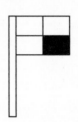

Which picture shows the flag after it has flipped?

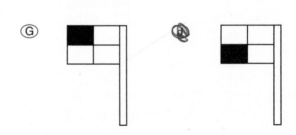

Ⓕ   Ⓗ

Ⓖ   Ⓙ

13. What time is shown on the clock?

Ⓐ 6:55
Ⓑ 10:25
Ⓒ 11:35
Ⓓ 12:35

GO ON ➡

Scholastic Inc.

Practice Test 6 *(continued)*

14. The floor of Lucy's rectangular bedroom is 14 feet long and 11 feet wide. What is the area of the floor?

Ⓕ 25 sq ft
Ⓖ 50 sq ft
Ⓗ 77 sq ft
Ⓙ 154 sq ft

15. A bag of 12 apples is most likely to weigh —

Ⓐ 2 ounces
Ⓑ 2 pounds
Ⓒ 2 grams
Ⓓ 2 tons

16. A truck driver drove 612 miles on Wednesday, 285 miles on Thursday, and 390 miles on Friday. <u>About</u> how far did he drive <u>all together</u>?

Ⓕ 900 miles
Ⓖ 1100 miles
Ⓗ 1300 miles
Ⓙ 1500 miles

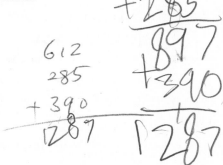

17. Mary has these coins in a purse. What is the value of the coins?

Ⓐ $0.75
Ⓑ $0.80
Ⓒ $0.90
Ⓓ $1.00

18. Leo started baking potatoes in the oven at 5:45 P.M. He took them out $1\frac{1}{2}$ hours later. Which clock shows the time he took the potatoes out of the oven?

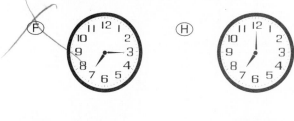

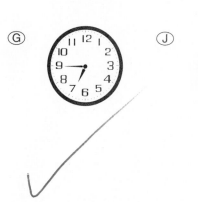

Practice Test 6 (continued)

19. How long is the salamander? (Use a centimeter ruler.)

This too

- Ⓐ 7 cm
- Ⓑ 6 cm
- Ⓒ 5 cm
- Ⓓ 4 cm

Don't have ruler

20. Timmy has 4 craft sticks. If he lays all 4 sticks end to end, what will be the total length? (Use an inch ruler.)

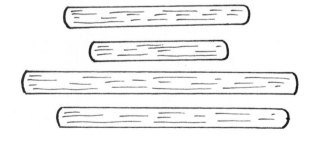

- Ⓕ 7 in.
- Ⓖ 8 in.
- Ⓗ 9 in.
- Ⓙ 10 in.

21. A bundle of roof shingles weighs 43 pounds. <u>About</u> how much will 17 bundles weigh?

- Ⓐ 400 lb
- Ⓒ 800 lb
- Ⓑ 600 lb
- Ⓓ 1000 lb

Maria went birdwatching on Saturday and kept track of how many different birds she saw. Use her tally chart to answer questions 22 and 23.

Birds Seen

Robins	‖‖ ‖‖	
Blue Jays	‖‖ ‖‖ ||||
Sparrows	‖‖ ‖‖ ‖‖ ‖‖ ||
Thrushes	‖‖ ‖‖ ||||
Warblers	‖‖ |||

22. How many warblers did Maria see?

- Ⓕ 14
- Ⓖ 13
- Ⓗ 9
- Ⓙ 8

23. Maria saw the same number of —

- Ⓐ robins and sparrows
- Ⓑ blue jays and thrushes
- Ⓒ robins and blue jays
- Ⓓ thrushes and sparrows

STOP

ANSWER SHEET

Practice Test # 6

Student Name _____ Grade _____

Teacher Name _____ Date _____

MATHEMATICS

1 Ⓐ Ⓑ Ⓒ Ⓓ Ⓔ	11 Ⓐ Ⓑ Ⓒ Ⓓ Ⓔ	21 Ⓐ Ⓑ Ⓒ Ⓓ Ⓔ	31 Ⓐ Ⓑ Ⓒ Ⓓ Ⓔ
2 Ⓕ Ⓖ Ⓗ Ⓙ Ⓚ	12 Ⓕ Ⓖ Ⓗ Ⓙ Ⓚ	22 Ⓕ Ⓖ Ⓗ Ⓙ Ⓚ	32 Ⓕ Ⓖ Ⓗ Ⓙ Ⓚ
3 Ⓐ Ⓑ Ⓒ Ⓓ Ⓔ	13 Ⓐ Ⓑ Ⓒ Ⓓ Ⓔ	23 Ⓐ Ⓑ Ⓒ Ⓓ Ⓔ	33 Ⓐ Ⓑ Ⓒ Ⓓ Ⓔ
4 Ⓕ Ⓖ Ⓗ Ⓙ Ⓚ	14 Ⓕ Ⓖ Ⓗ Ⓙ Ⓚ	24 Ⓕ Ⓖ Ⓗ Ⓙ Ⓚ	34 Ⓕ Ⓖ Ⓗ Ⓙ Ⓚ
5 Ⓐ Ⓑ Ⓒ Ⓓ Ⓔ	15 Ⓐ Ⓑ Ⓒ Ⓓ Ⓔ	25 Ⓐ Ⓑ Ⓒ Ⓓ Ⓔ	35 Ⓐ Ⓑ Ⓒ Ⓓ Ⓔ
6 Ⓕ Ⓖ Ⓗ Ⓙ Ⓚ	16 Ⓕ Ⓖ Ⓗ Ⓙ Ⓚ	26 Ⓕ Ⓖ Ⓗ Ⓙ Ⓚ	36 Ⓕ Ⓖ Ⓗ Ⓙ Ⓚ
7 Ⓐ Ⓑ Ⓒ Ⓓ Ⓔ	17 Ⓐ Ⓑ Ⓒ Ⓓ Ⓔ	27 Ⓐ Ⓑ Ⓒ Ⓓ Ⓔ	37 Ⓐ Ⓑ Ⓒ Ⓓ Ⓔ
8 Ⓕ Ⓖ Ⓗ Ⓙ Ⓚ	18 Ⓕ Ⓖ Ⓗ Ⓙ Ⓚ	28 Ⓕ Ⓖ Ⓗ Ⓙ Ⓚ	38 Ⓕ Ⓖ Ⓗ Ⓙ Ⓚ
9 Ⓐ Ⓑ Ⓒ Ⓓ Ⓔ	19 Ⓐ Ⓑ Ⓒ Ⓓ Ⓔ	29 Ⓐ Ⓑ Ⓒ Ⓓ Ⓔ	39 Ⓐ Ⓑ Ⓒ Ⓓ Ⓔ
10 Ⓕ Ⓖ Ⓗ Ⓙ Ⓚ	20 Ⓕ Ⓖ Ⓗ Ⓙ Ⓚ	30 Ⓕ Ⓖ Ⓗ Ⓙ Ⓚ	40 Ⓕ Ⓖ Ⓗ Ⓙ Ⓚ

Scholastic Inc.

Practice Test 7

Problem Solving

Name _____ Date _____

Practice Test 7

Directions. Choose the best answer to each question. Mark your answer. If the correct answer is *not given,* choose "NG."

1. The Jensons are driving from Buffalo to New York City. The distance is 419 miles. They have gone 250 miles so far. How many more miles do they have to go?

- (A) 159
- (B) 169
- (C) 229
- (D) 669
- (E) NG

2. A total of 95 students will march in a parade for Memorial Day. They will march in rows of 6 students per row. Which number sentence should you use to find how many rows of students there will be?

- (F) $95 \div 6 = \square$
- (G) $95 - 6 = \square$
- (H) $95 \times 6 = \square$
- (J) $95 + 6 = \square$
- (K) NG

3. In one hour, 74 cars went past a tollbooth. The driver of each car paid a $3.00 toll. How much money was collected in all?

- (A) $77.00
- (B) $212.00
- (C) $222.00
- (D) $252.00
- (E) NG

4. Jamie made 76 jars of pickles. If he puts 8 jars in a box, how many boxes will he need for 76 jars?

- (F) 7
- (G) 8
- (H) 9
- (J) 10
- (K) NG

5. Mrs. Grimes owned 11.6 acres of land. She sold 3.8 acres. How many acres of land does she have left?

- (A) 6.8
- (B) 7.3
- (C) 7.7
- (D) 8.8
- (E) NG

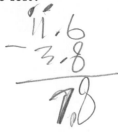

Name _____ Date _____

Practice Test 7 *(continued)*

6. Janelle bought this tool kit at a store. She gave the clerk a $20.00 bill.

How much change should she receive?
- (F) $4.23
- (G) $4.13
- (H) $4.03
- (J) $3.13
- (K) NG

20.00 − 15.87 = 4.13

7. The table shows the number of children in each grade at the Clark School.

Grade	Number of Children
1	104
2	85
3	92

How many children are there in all?
- (A) 270
- (B) 271
- (C) 280
- (D) 291
- (E) NG

8. Karen hiked all three trails shown on the map.

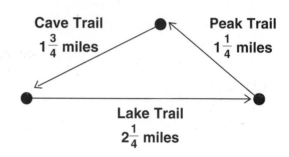

Cave Trail $1\frac{3}{4}$ miles
Peak Trail $1\frac{1}{4}$ miles
Lake Trail $2\frac{1}{4}$ miles

How far did she hike in all?
- (F) $5\frac{1}{4}$ miles
- (G) 5 miles
- (H) $4\frac{3}{4}$ miles
- (J) $4\frac{1}{4}$ miles
- (K) NG

9. Drew is 4 feet 4 inches tall. His brother Clancy is 3 feet 9 inches tall. How much taller is Drew?
- (A) 3 inches
- (B) 4 inches
- (C) 5 inches
- (D) 7 inches
- (E) NG

Practice Test 7 (continued)

10. A soccer game started at 2:45 P.M. It ended at 4:30 P.M. How long did the game last?

  Ⓕ 1 hr 15 min
  Ⓖ 1 hr 30 min
  Ⓗ 1 hr 45 min
  Ⓙ 2 hr 15 min
  Ⓚ NG

11. Rosa baby-sits for 24 hours each week. She baby-sat for 6 hours on Sunday and 4 hours on Wednesday. How many more hours does she have to baby-sit?

  Ⓐ 14
  Ⓑ 18
  Ⓒ 20
  Ⓓ 34
  Ⓔ NG

12. Liam traveled for 4 weeks and 4 days. How many days is that all together?

  Ⓕ 24
  Ⓖ 28
  Ⓗ 30
  Ⓙ 36
  Ⓚ NG

13. A pea plant is 16 inches tall. It grows 3 inches per week. At this rate, how tall will the plant be in 3 weeks?

  Ⓐ 19 in.
  Ⓑ 22 in.
  Ⓒ 25 in.
  Ⓓ 28 in.
  Ⓔ NG

14. Mike ran 32 miles last week. Shem ran 26 miles. Which number sentence should you use to find how many more miles Mike ran?

  Ⓕ $32 - 26 = \square$
  Ⓖ $32 \div 26 = \square$
  Ⓗ $26 - 32 = \square$
  Ⓙ $26 + 32 = \square$
  Ⓚ NG

15. Lynne started playing basketball at 4:30 P.M. She played for 40 minutes. At what time did she stop playing?

  Ⓐ 5:00 P.M.
  Ⓑ 5:10 P.M.
  Ⓒ 5:20 P.M.
  Ⓓ 5:40 P.M.
  Ⓔ NG

GO ON

Scholastic Inc.

Practice Test 7 *(continued)*

16. If you spin this spinner 10 times, which number will the spinner probably land on most often?

Ⓕ 3
Ⓖ 4
Ⓗ 6
Ⓙ 7
Ⓚ NG

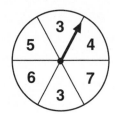

17. A toy store has a large bin of yo-yos. The chart shows how many yo-yos of each color are in the bin.

Color	Number
White	35
Orange	42
Pink	30
Green	54
Black	46

If you reach into the bin without looking and take one yo-yo, which color are you most likely to get?

Ⓐ orange
Ⓑ pink
Ⓒ green
Ⓓ black
Ⓔ NG

18. Mr. Crowley was painting the windows on his house. It took 5 hours to paint 3 windows. At this rate, how long would it take to paint 18 windows?

Ⓕ 21 hours
Ⓖ 24 hours
Ⓗ 27 hours
Ⓙ 30 hours
Ⓚ NG

19. Hannah had $100.00. She spent $64.00 on food and $28.00 for books. How much did she have left?

Ⓐ $6.00
Ⓑ $8.00
Ⓒ $18.00
Ⓓ $32.00
Ⓔ NG

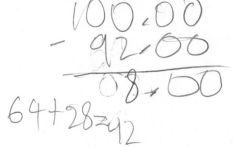

20. Steve earned $875 during the summer. Mandy earned $160 more than Steve. How much did Mandy earn?

Ⓕ $715
Ⓖ $935
Ⓗ $985
Ⓙ $1025
Ⓚ NG

GO ON

Scholastic Inc.

Practice Test 7 (continued)

Excellent!

21. Stan made a tower of 5 blocks. The yellow block is at the bottom. The red block is between the blue and white blocks. The green block is below the white block but above the yellow block. Which color block is at the top of the tower?

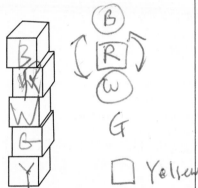

Ⓐ red
Ⓑ green
Ⓒ white
Ⓓ blue
Ⓔ NG

22. Amy is making 80 cookies for a bake sale. She made 36 cookies in one batch and 28 cookies in another batch. How many more cookies does she need to make?

Ⓕ 12
Ⓖ 16
Ⓗ 26
Ⓙ 64
Ⓚ NG

23. A 4th-grade class went to the Nature Center on a field trip. They spent a total of $124 for tickets. What else do you need to know to figure out how much each ticket cost?

Ⓐ where the Nature Center was
Ⓑ what day the trip took place
Ⓒ the name of the Nature Center
Ⓓ how many students went on the trip

24. Saul makes $19 an hour at his job. **About** how much will he earn in 28 hours?

Ⓕ $30–$40
Ⓖ $50–$60
Ⓗ $300–$400
Ⓙ $500–$600

25. A factory made 1130 brooms on Monday, 2940 brooms on Tuesday, and 1800 brooms on Wednesday. **About** how many brooms were made in all?

Ⓐ 8000
Ⓑ 7000
Ⓒ 6000
Ⓓ 5000

STOP

Scholastic Inc.

ANSWER SHEET

Practice Test # 7

Student Name _____ Grade _____

Teacher Name _____ Date _____

MATHEMATICS

1 (A) (B) (C) (D) (E)   11 (A) (B) (C) (D) (E)   21 (A) (B) (C) (D) (E)   31 (A) (B) (C) (D) (E)

2 (F) (G) (H) (J) (K)   12 (F) (G) (H) (J) (K)   22 (F) (G) (H) (J) (K)   32 (F) (G) (H) (J) (K)

3 (A) (B) (C) (D) (E)   13 (A) (B) (C) (D) (E)   23 (A) (B) (C) (D) (E)   33 (A) (B) (C) (D) (E)

4 (F) (G) (H) (J) (K)   14 (F) (G) (H) (J) (K)   24 (F) (G) (H) (J) (K)   34 (F) (G) (H) (J) (K)

5 (A) (B) (C) (D) (E)   15 (A) (B) (C) (D) (E)   25 (A) (B) (C) (D) (E)   35 (A) (B) (C) (D) (E)

6 (F) (G) (H) (J) (K)   16 (F) (G) (H) (J) (K)   26 (F) (G) (H) (J) (K)   36 (F) (G) (H) (J) (K)

7 (A) (B) (C) (D) (E)   17 (A) (B) (C) (D) (E)   27 (A) (B) (C) (D) (E)   37 (A) (B) (C) (D) (E)

8 (F) (G) (H) (J) (K)   18 (F) (G) (H) (J) (K)   28 (F) (G) (H) (J) (K)   38 (F) (G) (H) (J) (K)

9 (A) (B) (C) (D) (E)   19 (A) (B) (C) (D) (E)   29 (A) (B) (C) (D) (E)   39 (A) (B) (C) (D) (E)

10 (F) (G) (H) (J) (K)   20 (F) (G) (H) (J) (K)   30 (F) (G) (H) (J) (K)   40 (F) (G) (H) (J) (K)

Practice Test 8

Computation

Practice Test 8

Directions. Choose the best answer to each question. Mark your answer. If the correct answer is *not given,* choose "NG."

1.
$$\begin{array}{r} 195 \\ 76 \\ + 538 \\ \hline \end{array}$$
809

   Ⓐ 819
   Ⓑ 809
   Ⓒ 808
   Ⓓ 709
   Ⓔ NG

2.
$$\begin{array}{r} 304 \\ - 92 \\ \hline 212 \end{array}$$

   Ⓕ 202
   Ⓖ 206
   Ⓗ 212
   Ⓙ 396
   Ⓚ NG

3.
$$\begin{array}{r} 571 \\ - 238 \\ \hline 333 \end{array}$$

   Ⓐ 333
   Ⓑ 343
   Ⓒ 347
   Ⓓ 809
   Ⓔ NG

4. This chart shows the number of students who visited the school nurse each day.

Visits to the School Nurse	
Tuesday	11
Wednesday	15
Thursday	16
Friday	18

What was the average number of students who visited the school nurse each day?

   Ⓕ 12
   Ⓖ 14
   Ⓗ 16
   Ⓙ 60
   Ⓚ NG

5. This chart shows the number of people who went to an art show each day.

Day	Number of Visitors
Thursday	271
Friday	328
Saturday	406

How many people went to the art show in all?

   Ⓐ 905
   Ⓑ 995
   Ⓒ 1005
   Ⓓ 1015
   Ⓔ NG

GO ON ➡

Practice Test 8 *(continued)*

6.
36
× 5
(written: 180)

- Ⓕ 41
- Ⓖ 150
- Ⓗ 170
- Ⓙ 180 ⭕
- Ⓚ NG

7.
208
× 4
(written: 832)

- Ⓐ 872
- Ⓑ 832 ⭕
- Ⓒ 632
- Ⓓ 212
- Ⓔ NG

8.
70
× 30

- Ⓕ 100
- Ⓖ 210
- Ⓗ 2100 ⭕
- Ⓙ 2900
- Ⓚ NG

9. 7 × ☐ = 42

- Ⓐ 5
- Ⓑ 7
- Ⓒ 8
- Ⓓ 9
- Ⓔ NG ⭕

10. Pilar has 3 different colored skirts and 5 different blouses.

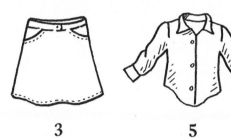

3   5

How many different combinations of one skirt and one blouse can she make?

- Ⓕ 8
- Ⓖ 10
- Ⓗ 15 ⭕
- Ⓙ 16
- Ⓚ NG

11. Cal has these loose socks in a drawer.

Color	Number
Blue	6
White	7
Brown	8
Black	3

If Cal takes one sock out of the drawer without looking, what is the probability that he will get a brown sock?

- Ⓐ $\frac{1}{3}$ ⭕
- Ⓑ $\frac{1}{24}$
- Ⓒ $\frac{1}{4}$
- Ⓓ $\frac{1}{6}$
- Ⓔ NG

GO ON

Name _____ Date _____

Practice Test 8 *(continued)*

12. $36 \div 4 =$

Ⓕ 6
Ⓖ 7
Ⓗ 8
Ⓙ 9
Ⓚ NG

13. $8\overline{)64}$

Ⓐ 6
Ⓑ 7
Ⓒ 8
Ⓓ 9
Ⓔ NG

14. $3\overline{)96}$

Ⓕ 30
Ⓖ 31
Ⓗ 33
Ⓙ 320
Ⓚ NG

15. $4\overline{)800}$

Ⓐ 240
Ⓑ 220
Ⓒ 210
Ⓓ 22
Ⓔ NG

16. The grid map shows where five towns are located.

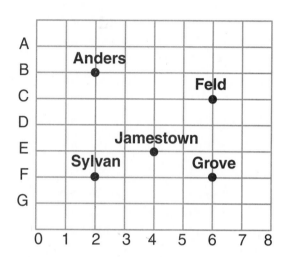

Which town is located at 4E?

Ⓕ Jamestown
Ⓖ Anders
Ⓗ Grove
Ⓙ Sylvan
Ⓚ NG

17. Mr. Graves wrote this number sentence on the blackboard.

$(12 + n) - 8 = 20$

What is the value of n?

Ⓐ 4
Ⓑ 12
Ⓒ 16
Ⓓ 28
Ⓔ NG

GO ON

Scholastic Inc.

Practice Test 8 *(continued)*

18. This chart lists the number of cars sold by Auto Shop in each of 4 months.

Vehicles Sold	
May	12
June	10
July	16
August	14

What was the average number of cars sold per month?

- Ⓕ 52
- Ⓖ 14
- Ⓗ 13
- Ⓙ 12
- Ⓚ NG

19. Leanne wrote this number sentence to solve a problem.

$$(6 \times n) - 10 = 20$$

What is the value of *n*?

- Ⓐ 30
- Ⓑ 8
- Ⓒ 6
- Ⓓ 5
- Ⓔ NG

The grid below shows the location of five points. Use the grid to answer questions 20 and 21.

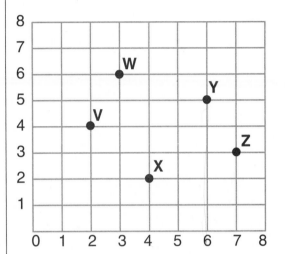

20. What point is located at (4, 2)?

- Ⓕ W
- Ⓖ X
- Ⓗ Y
- Ⓙ Z
- Ⓚ NG

21. What is the location of point Y?

- Ⓐ (5, 6)
- Ⓑ (7, 3)
- Ⓒ (2, 4)
- Ⓓ (3, 6)
- Ⓔ NG

GO ON

Practice Test 8 *(continued)*

22. $\dfrac{3}{10} + \dfrac{9}{10} =$

⒡ $\dfrac{10}{12}$

⒢ $\dfrac{12}{20}$

⒣ $\dfrac{3}{5}$

ⓙ $1\dfrac{1}{5}$

⒦ NG

23.
$$\dfrac{5}{8}$$
$$+ \dfrac{3}{8}$$

Ⓐ $\dfrac{1}{4}$

Ⓑ $\dfrac{7}{8}$

Ⓒ $\dfrac{3}{4}$

Ⓓ 1

Ⓔ NG

24.
$$\dfrac{5}{9}$$
$$- \dfrac{4}{9}$$

⒡ $\dfrac{1}{9}$

⒢ $\dfrac{9}{18}$

⒣ $\dfrac{1}{4}$

ⓙ 1

⒦ NG

25. $6.3 + 4.5 =$

Ⓐ 1.8

Ⓑ 10.2

Ⓒ 10.6

Ⓓ 11.8

Ⓔ NG

10.8

26. $14.85 + 7.7 =$

⒡ 23.55

⒢ 22.55

⒣ 22.25

ⓙ 7.15

⒦ NG

27.
$$\$28.50$$
$$- \ 19.95$$

Ⓐ $8.55

Ⓑ $11.45

Ⓒ $18.55

Ⓓ $48.45

Ⓔ NG

28. $26.04 - 18.9 =$

⒡ 7.05

⒢ 7.14

⒣ 8.5

ⓙ 44.94

⒦ NG

STOP

Scholastic Inc.

ANSWER SHEET

Student Name _____ Grade _____

Teacher Name _____ Date _____

MATHEMATICS

1 Ⓐ Ⓑ Ⓒ Ⓓ Ⓔ	11 Ⓐ Ⓑ Ⓒ Ⓓ Ⓔ	21 Ⓐ Ⓑ Ⓒ Ⓓ Ⓔ	31 Ⓐ Ⓑ Ⓒ Ⓓ Ⓔ
2 Ⓕ Ⓖ Ⓗ Ⓙ Ⓚ	12 Ⓕ Ⓖ Ⓗ Ⓙ Ⓚ	22 Ⓕ Ⓖ Ⓗ Ⓙ Ⓚ	32 Ⓕ Ⓖ Ⓗ Ⓙ Ⓚ
3 Ⓐ Ⓑ Ⓒ Ⓓ Ⓔ	13 Ⓐ Ⓑ Ⓒ Ⓓ Ⓔ	23 Ⓐ Ⓑ Ⓒ Ⓓ Ⓔ	33 Ⓐ Ⓑ Ⓒ Ⓓ Ⓔ
4 Ⓕ Ⓖ Ⓗ Ⓙ Ⓚ	14 Ⓕ Ⓖ Ⓗ Ⓙ Ⓚ	24 Ⓕ Ⓖ Ⓗ Ⓙ Ⓚ	34 Ⓕ Ⓖ Ⓗ Ⓙ Ⓚ
5 Ⓐ Ⓑ Ⓒ Ⓓ Ⓔ	15 Ⓐ Ⓑ Ⓒ Ⓓ Ⓔ	25 Ⓐ Ⓑ Ⓒ Ⓓ Ⓔ	35 Ⓐ Ⓑ Ⓒ Ⓓ Ⓔ
6 Ⓕ Ⓖ Ⓗ Ⓙ Ⓚ	16 Ⓕ Ⓖ Ⓗ Ⓙ Ⓚ	26 Ⓕ Ⓖ Ⓗ Ⓙ Ⓚ	36 Ⓕ Ⓖ Ⓗ Ⓙ Ⓚ
7 Ⓐ Ⓑ Ⓒ Ⓓ Ⓔ	17 Ⓐ Ⓑ Ⓒ Ⓓ Ⓔ	27 Ⓐ Ⓑ Ⓒ Ⓓ Ⓔ	37 Ⓐ Ⓑ Ⓒ Ⓓ Ⓔ
8 Ⓕ Ⓖ Ⓗ Ⓙ Ⓚ	18 Ⓕ Ⓖ Ⓗ Ⓙ Ⓚ	28 Ⓕ Ⓖ Ⓗ Ⓙ Ⓚ	38 Ⓕ Ⓖ Ⓗ Ⓙ Ⓚ
9 Ⓐ Ⓑ Ⓒ Ⓓ Ⓔ	19 Ⓐ Ⓑ Ⓒ Ⓓ Ⓔ	29 Ⓐ Ⓑ Ⓒ Ⓓ Ⓔ	39 Ⓐ Ⓑ Ⓒ Ⓓ Ⓔ
10 Ⓕ Ⓖ Ⓗ Ⓙ Ⓚ	20 Ⓕ Ⓖ Ⓗ Ⓙ Ⓚ	30 Ⓕ Ⓖ Ⓗ Ⓙ Ⓚ	40 Ⓕ Ⓖ Ⓗ Ⓙ Ⓚ

Practice Test 1 Tested Skills	Item Numbers
MATHEMATICS (1–28)	
Numeration and Number Concepts	
Associate numerals and number words	1, 19
Compare and order whole numbers	3, 10, 11
Use place value and rounding	5, 12, 13, 21, 22
Identify number patterns	7, 9, 17, 20
Estimation	15, 23
Factoring	18
Identify fractional parts	4, 8, 28
Compare and order fractions	6, 27
Apply operational properties (zero, addition/subtraction, commutative property)	2, 14, 16, 24, 25, 26

Practice Test 2 Tested Skills	Item Numbers
MATHEMATICS (1–22)	
Geometry and Measurement	
Identify plane and solid figures and their parts	1, 2
Recognize symmetry and congruence	5
Identify lines (intersecting, parallel)	3, 4
Identify transformations	6
Find perimeter and area	7, 8
Recognize money	9
Tell time	10, 11
Identify appropriate units of measurement	12, 13
Use measurement instruments (rulers, thermometer)	14, 15, 16
Estimate measurements	17, 18
Interpret bar graphs, tables, charts	19, 20, 21, 22

Practice Test 3 Tested Skills	Item Numbers
MATHEMATICS (1–25)	
Problem Solving	
Solve one-step problems using basic operations	1, 3, 4, 5, 8, 24
Solve problems involving money, time, measurement	6, 7, 9, 11, 12, 15
Solve problems involving estimation and ratio/proportion	13, 18, 21, 22
Solve problems involving probability and logic	16, 17, 19
Identify steps in solving problems	2, 14, 23
Solve multi-step problems	10, 20, 25

Practice Test 4 Tested Skills	Item Numbers
MATHEMATICS (1–28)	
Computation	
Add and subtract whole numbers	1, 2, 3, 5
Multiply whole numbers	6, 7, 8, 9
Divide whole numbers	12, 13, 14, 15
Add and subtract fractions	22, 23, 24
Add and subtract decimals	25, 26, 27, 28
Find average, probability, and combinations	4, 10, 11, 18
Solve simple equations	17, 19
Find coordinates on a grid	16, 20, 21

Practice Test 5 Tested Skills	Item Numbers
MATHEMATICS (1–28)	
Numeration and Number Concepts	
Associate numerals and number words	1, 19
Compare and order whole numbers	3, 10, 11
Use place value and rounding	5, 12, 13, 21, 22
Identify patterns	7, 9, 17, 20
Estimation	15, 23
Factoring	18, 25
Identify fractional parts	4, 8, 26
Compare and order fractions	6, 27
Apply operational properties (zero, addition/subtraction, commutative property)	2, 14, 16, 24, 28

Practice Test 6 Tested Skills	Item Numbers
MATHEMATICS (1–23)	
Geometry and Measurement	
Identify plane and solid figures and their parts	1, 2, 3
Recognize symmetry and congruence	4, 9
Identify lines (intersecting, parallel)	5, 6
Identify transformations	12
Find perimeter and area	10, 14
Recognize money	17
Tell time	13, 18
Identify appropriate units of measurement	11, 15
Use measurement instruments	19, 20
Estimate measurements	16, 21
Interpret bar graphs, tables, charts	7, 8, 22, 23

Practice Test 7 Tested Skills	Item Numbers
MATHEMATICS (1–25)	
Problem Solving	
Solve one-step problems using basic operations	1, 3, 4, 5, 7, 20
Solve problems involving money, time, measurement	6, 8, 9, 10, 12, 15
Solve problems involving estimation and ratio/proportion	13, 18, 24, 25
Solve problems involving probability and logic	16, 17, 21
Identify steps in solving problems	2, 14, 23
Solve multi-step problems	11, 19, 22

Practice Test 8 Tested Skills	Item Numbers
MATHEMATICS (1–28)	
Computation	
Add and subtract whole numbers	1, 2, 3, 5
Multiply whole numbers	6, 7, 8, 9
Divide whole numbers	12, 13, 14, 15
Add and subtract fractions	22, 23, 24
Add and subtract decimals	25, 26, 27, 28
Find average, probability, and combinations	4, 10, 11, 18
Solve simple equations	17, 19
Find coordinates on a grid	16, 20, 21

ANSWER KEY

Practice Test 1
MATHEMATICS
Numeration and
Number Concepts

1.	C	15.	D
2.	G	16.	F
3.	B	17.	B
4.	J	18.	H
5.	C	19.	A
6.	J	20.	J
7.	D	21.	B
8.	F	22.	G
9.	B	23.	D
10.	J	24.	J
11.	A	25.	B
12.	G	26.	H
13.	C	27.	B
14.	H	28.	F

Practice Test 2
MATHEMATICS
Geometry and
Measurement

1.	C	12.	G
2.	G	13.	A
3.	B	14.	J
4.	F	15.	C
5.	D	16.	H
6.	H	17.	D
7.	B	18.	G
8.	H	19.	C
9.	D	20.	G
10.	J	21.	D
11.	C	22.	F

Practice Test 3
MATHEMATICS
Problem Solving

1.	B	14.	K
2.	J	15.	D
3.	C	16.	F
4.	H	17.	C
5.	E	18.	J
6.	G	19.	A
7.	E	20.	F
8.	J	21.	C
9.	C	22.	H
10.	J	23.	A
11.	B	24.	G
12.	H	25.	B
13.	D		

Practice Test 4
MATHEMATICS
Computation

1.	D	15.	D
2.	K	16.	J
3.	C	17.	A
4.	G	18.	H
5.	B	19.	E
6.	J	20.	G
7.	E	21.	D
8.	H	22.	H
9.	C	23.	A
10.	G	24.	G
11.	A	25.	B
12.	K	26.	K
13.	C	27.	D
14.	G	28.	J

Practice Test 5
MATHEMATICS
Numeration and
Number Concepts

1.	B	15.	D
2.	F	16.	G
3.	D	17.	B
4.	H	18.	F
5.	C	19.	B
6.	G	20.	H
7.	A	21.	D
8.	J	22.	H
9.	C	23.	C
10.	G	24.	F
11.	D	25.	A
12.	H	26.	G
13.	C	27.	A
14.	J	28.	J

Practice Test 6
MATHEMATICS
Geometry and
Measurement

1.	B	13.	C
2.	J	14.	J
3.	A	15.	B
4.	F	16.	H
5.	B	17.	D
6.	H	18.	F
7.	C	19.	A
8.	H	20.	H
9.	A	21.	C
10.	G	22.	J
11.	D	23.	B
12.	J		

Practice Test 7
MATHEMATICS
Problem Solving

1.	B	14.	F
2.	F	15.	B
3.	C	16.	F
4.	J	17.	C
5.	E	18.	J
6.	G	19.	B
7.	E	20.	K
8.	F	21.	D
9.	D	22.	G
10.	H	23.	D
11.	A	24.	J
12.	K	25.	C
13.	C		

Practice Test 8
MATHEMATICS
Computation

1.	B	15.	E
2.	H	16.	F
3.	A	17.	C
4.	K	18.	H
5.	C	19.	D
6.	J	20.	G
7.	B	21.	E
8.	H	22.	J
9.	E	23.	D
10.	H	24.	F
11.	A	25.	E
12.	J	26.	G
13.	C	27.	A
14.	K	28.	G